Two Trees

By MARILYN FRANSHAM

PHOTOGRAPHY *by* ROD CARTASEGNA

*Keep Believing!
Love Marilyn Fransham*

ARNICA PUBLISHING, INC.
Portland, Oregon

I dedicate this to Mark and
our everlasting love.

I thank Arnica for their healing strength and for
believing in the shining courage of this world.

Big hugs to my Shelly and Jazzie and
all my little ones.

And a big hug to all my family and friends
around the world and all the trees that unite us.

Text © 2010 by Marilyn Fransham
Photographs © 2010 by Rod Cartasegna

All rights reserved. No part of this book may be reproduced or transmitted in any form or by any means, electronic or mechanical, including photocopying, recording, or by any information storage and retrieval system, without written permission of the publisher.

Library of Congress Cataloging-in-Publication Data

Fransham, Marilyn, 1958-
 Two trees / by Marilyn Fransham ; photography by Rod Cartasegna.
    p. cm.
 ISBN 978-0-9816822-3-5 (hardcover)
 1. Conduct of life. I. Title.
 BJ1597.F73 2010
 170'.44—dc22
                    2010036571

Arnica Publishing
3880 SE Eighth Ave., Suite 110
Portland, Oregon 97202

CEO/Founder: Ross Hawkins
Board Chair: Diane Vines
Production Director: Dick Owsiany
Design: Vicki Knapton

Editorial Team:
Michelle McCann, developmental editor
Kathy Howard, managing editor

Once there was a tiny tree.

She grew beside a sparkling stream in a big forest. That little tree was so anxious to grow. She wanted to stand tall like the other trees around her. She longed to see her reflection spanning out over the water that flowed beneath the strong bank.

𝒴*ears* passed.

    Rain watered the soil around her, sunlight warmed her needles, and the little tree grew.

    She grew and her roots and trunk became strong. She grew until she could reach out her branches and touch the trees around her.

One moonlit evening, the tree realized she had finally grown tall enough to see herself mirrored in the ripples of the stream. A star was shining brightly at the top of her crown.

She was not such a little tree anymore.

The tree's dreams were becoming realities. She had grown into everything she ever wanted to be.

This made her happy.

Not only did the little tree grow big and beautiful, she found she had many purposes.

Animals played beneath her. Some climbed around her trunk. Birds built nests upon her branches. This tree was strong and weathered the seasons.

Even people came upon her on their walks in the big forest. They sat under her wide limbs, relaxing for a while. They admired her beauty and her strength. They shared precious moments beneath the boughs of this great tree.

𝒲𝒽𝑒𝓃 people came, the tree stood quietly and listened to them, young and old, telling their stories. They talked of many things, but a few talked about how beauty comes from within.

The tree listened closely. She heard them say that inner beauty grows with age and is the greatest gift of all.

She was happy with how tall she had grown and how strong her branches were. The tree thought she could feel the strength of her core. She wondered how strong she would grow to be.

She wondered if this was what they meant by inner beauty.

Then, one year, the wind and cold came in like never before, and they took their toll on the mighty tree.

Her green needles sagged. Her strong branches drooped. She grew weak and began to shed her outer beauty.

As her needles and bark fell away, the tree was exposed and vulnerable.

She tried to regain her strength, but it was so hard.

This once majestic tree crashed to the ground.

She lay there with only some of her roots intact.

$\mathcal{B}eside$ the great, fallen tree grew a tiny sprout.

He was small and just beginning to reach up toward the sun. The great tree remembered being just like him, innocent and anxious, yet so strong and full of life.

The great tree wondered why we all seem to be created with so little wisdom. She wondered if she shared her stories and experiences with this little tree, would that help him as he grew?

She decided her wisdom would help him. So she began to share the tales of her life with the little tree.

The little tree listened and he did appreciate all that she shared with him. Her wisdom helped him grow and appreciate his life and the life around him. Through her stories and her kindness he began to see what was inside her.

The little tree grew to love the inner beauty of this great tree.

So he reached out his strong, healthy limbs and intertwined with the branches of the fallen tree.

Many winters passed, cloaking the little tree and the great fallen tree in blankets of snow, draping them in icicles like diamonds.

Each spring brought sun and rain and new buds to the trees.

And all the while, the big tree told her stories and the little tree listened and grew.

𝒥n the summers, the sun warmed their needles and gave them strength. The autumns toughened the two trees.

Through all the seasons and all the years, the big tree told her stories and the little tree listened and grew.

Then one day the wise old tree looked around and discovered that she was upright once again. She was standing side by side with the little tree.

Only he was not such a little tree anymore.

The great old tree could see how beautiful they were together. The sun lit up their bright green needles. They were healthy and abundant with ornamental pinecones. Rabbits, squirrels, and chipmunks played around their trunks. Little birds nestled in their branches like corsages. People stopped and marveled at this natural wonder.

$\mathcal{T}he$ old tree understood that outer beauty can easily fall away.

It was their inner beauty that awed her. She could see her own inner strength and courage. She could see his inner strength and courage.

They learned so much from each other and from the lives of those around them. And they were happy. They could see the beauty inside them was everlasting. They humbly wanted to share with others what they had learned.